# YING TONG

First published in this play in 2004 by Oberon Books Ltd
Electronic edition published in 2013

Oberon Books Ltd
521 Caledonian Road, London N7 9RH
Tel: +44 (0) 20 7607 3637 / Fax: +44 (0) 20 7607 3629
e-mail: info@oberonbooks.com
www.oberonbooks.com

A catalogue record for this book is available from the British
Library.

PB ISBN: 978-1-84002-525-5
E ISBN: 978-1-78319-389-9

eBook conversion by Replika Press PVT Ltd, India.

Visit www.oberonbooks.com to read more about all our books
and to buy them. You will also find features, author interviews and
news of any author events, and you can sign up for e-newsletters
so that you're always first to hear about our new releases.

# CHARACTERS

SPIKE MILLIGAN
a comedian/writer in his early forties

PETER SELLERS
a comedian in his thirties

HARRY SECOMBE
a comedian in his thirties

WALLACE GREENSLADE
a BBC announcer in his late forties

## Music:
'Crazy Rhythm'
'The Ying Tong Song'
'We'll Keep A Welcome In The Hillsides'
'Little White Bull'

# Ying Tong
## By Roy Smiles

First performance: Courtyard Theatre, West Yorkshire Playhouse, Friday 22 October 2004

The cast was as follows:

| | |
|---|---|
| Jeremy Child | Wallace Greenslade |
| James Clyde | Spike Milligan |
| Christian Patterson | Harry Secombe |
| Peter Temple | Peter Sellers |

| | |
|---|---|
| *Director* | Michael Kingsbury |
| *Designer* | Peter McKintosh |
| *Composer* | Richard Taylor |
| *Lighting Designer* | Tony Simpson |
| *Sound Designer* | Mic Pool |
| *Voice* | Penny Dyer |
| *Casting* | Sam Jones CDG |

| | |
|---|---|
| *Deputy Stage Manager* | Sally McKenna |

*Dedicated to:*
*My brother Paul – a Goon in the room next door.*


*Thanks to:*
*Terry Johnson, Michael Kingsbury, Michael Codron,*
*Moira Mooney, Rachel Hughes, Sheila Ferber,*
*Mike 'Fluffy' Kemp, all at West Yorkshire Playhouse and my*
*son Sam for keeping me sane*
*during the writing of this play.*

# ACT ONE

*A bare white-walled stage empty save for a metal framed hospital bed, an upright chair and nurse's desk downstage and right of this; two doors: far left and far right.*

*At the front of the stage four microphones stamped 'BBC' hang down from above. These rise or fall dependent on whether a scene is set in a radio theatre.*

*Music: the 'Crazy Rhythm' theme.*

*As the lights rise Wallace GREENSLADE, Peter SELLERS, Spike MILLIGAN and Harry SECOMBE stand at microphones. Scripts in hand. A Goon Show, we presume, is about to begin.*

GREENSLADE: This is the BBC Home Service.

SELLERS: (*Bloodnok voice.*) They'll never take me alive I tell you!

GREENSLADE: Once more with feeling: this is the BBC Home Service.

MILLIGAN: (*Yells.*) Abandon license fee! Women and children first!

GREENSLADE: Yes, for the last time this evening at popular prices, that unacceptable face of sadism: the Goon Show.

*FX: mass booing from football terraces.*

GREENSLADE: How vulgar the common swineherd.

SECOMBE: Don't talk about BBC producers that way, Wal. You know they bear a grudge.

GREENSLADE: I shall grovel later. But to our sorry tale. Episode One: War & Peas. Somewhere midst the windswept hovels of Swansea, a myopic blubber of fat from Wales, attempting to support his illegal addiction to meat pasties, sells second-hand leeks to passing charabancs.

SECOMBE: (*Sings to the tune of 'Who Will Buy'.*)
'Who will buy a second hand leek, boy?
Such a leek I never did see.
Who will buy a second hand leek, boy?
And stuff it in their gob for me?'

SELLERS: (*Bluebottle voice.*) Would you mind taking your hand out of your pocket whilst you warble please, genial Seagoon person? I'm trying to pick it. For I am thruppence short for my wine-gums.

SECOMBE: Bluebottle!

SELLERS: (*Bluebottle voice.*) Yes, it is I. Strikes defiant Alan Ladd pose and waits for spontaneous wave of audience love. Not a thing. Sheds a silent tear.

SECOMBE: But – wait – what are you doing waving that white flag?

SELLERS: (*Bluebottle voice.*) Surrendering. I am a conscientious objector from the boy scout movement. They've stripped me of my woggle: the dirty rotten swines.

SECOMBE: Why are you surrendering from the boy scout movement?

SELLERS: (*Bluebottle voice.*) I started a camp fire by rubbing two sticks repeatedly against my knees. It set light to my legs.

SECOMBE: Ye Gads! What happened?

SELLERS: (*Bluebottle voice.*) They had to beat out the flames with a girl guide. Yet they still refused to give me my pyromaniac badge. The scout movement are lions led by donkeys I tell you. I curse the day I ever dobbed my dib.

SECOMBE: How fascinating yet at the same time tedious. But who's that jabbering ninny idly warming marshmallows on the dying embers of your kneecaps?

SELLERS: (*Bluebottle voice.*) Why that's my very good friend Eccles. Tee-hee.

MILLIGAN: (*Eccles voice.*) Hello there!

SECOMBE: Eccles, eh? I observed a man who but for a village would be its idiot. Tell me, young imbecile –

MILLIGAN: (*Eccles voice.*) Who you calling an imbecile? I got a diploma from borstal.

SECOMBE: What in?

MILLIGAN: (*Eccles voice.*) Stealing.

SECOMBE: I know I'm going to hate myself in the morning for asking this but: what are you doing with that camel?

MILLIGAN: (*Eccles voice.*) Smoking it.

SECOMBE: Put that dromedary down, man. You don't know where it's been.

MILLIGAN: (*Eccles voice.*) I've cut down – to only three hundred a day.

SECOMBE: That's not a cigarette, you nit. That's a ship of the desert.

MILLIGAN: (*Eccles voice.*) I wondered why it tasted funny.

SECOMBE: A packet of twenty must be hell to pick up.

MILLIGAN: (*Eccles voice.*) It's catching them when you put the match up to their bottoms that's the problem.

GREENSLADE: Author's note: no matches were actually harmed in the making of this radio programme.

SELLERS: (*Bluebottle voice.*) 'Ere, my good friend Eccles, can I borrow your camel? I have decided to forsake civilised society and join the French Foreign Legion; which is the boy scout movement with guns – and a sneer. So I can be beastly to the Bedouin.

SECOMBE: Do you speak French?

SELLERS: (*Bluebottle voice.*) Au contraire.

SECOMBE: How will you make yourself understood?

SELLERS: (*Bluebottle voice.*) Easy. You tickle its hump to turn right or thump its hump to turn left. Tee-hee. (sings.) 'Take my hand – I'm a stranger in Paradise!' Go on, Eccles, you dirty rotten swine, lend me your filthy, rotten camel.

*A long silence from MILLIGAN. The others swap worried glances. Glancing at their scripts.*

GREENSLADE: Spike? It's your line.

SELLERS: Eccles? (*louder.*) Lend me your filthy, rotten camel.

SECOMBE: Spike?

*Another awkward silence. MILLIGAN attempts to speak but no words come out of his mouth save for a vague gargling sound. He then mutters frantic, incoherent gibberish and starts to try to tear his script in half with his bare hands. Getting nowhere with that he drops his script and starts jumping up and down on it with extreme violence; tearing at his hair and clothes like a deranged banshee.*

SELLERS: (*Appalled.*) My God – he's finally gone gaga.

*A snap blackout.*

*Music: a rabidly speeded-up version of 'The Ying Tong Song.'*

*When the lights rise MILLIGAN sits up in bed with a sheet over his head. Three of the microphones have disappeared. GREENSLADE stands at the remaining microphone wearing a doctor's jacket. The music fades. We hear the sound of typing from under the sheet. GREENSLADE speaks into the microphone to audience:*

GREENSLADE: St Luke's psychiatric hospital, 1960. The wards teeming with new inmates due to Tommy Steele being number one in the Hit Parade with *Little White Bull.* God help us each and every one.

*GREENSLADE crosses to where MILLIGAN is in bed. He pulls back the sheet. We find MILLIGAN typing slowly but relentlessly on a tiny portable typewriter. He looks up at GREENSLADE and stops typing.*

How are you feeling today, Mr Milligan?

MILLIGAN: Suicidal thank you.

GREENSLADE: An improvement on yesterday then?

MILLIGAN: (*Frowns.*) It is?

GREENSLADE: I'd better take that.

*GREENSLADE takes away the typewriter and places it on the nurse's desk.*

You're here to rest. Over-work was the cause of your breakdown in the first place.

MILLIGAN: But I have to write. The BBC make me you see. All year – every year. Regardless of how ill I am. It's persecution. That's what it is. They'll not be happy 'til I'm dead. Or writing for ITV. Which is worse.

GREENSLADE: Nonsense. I'm sure the BBC have your best welfare at heart. They're not monsters after all.

MILLIGAN: (*Genuine surprise.*) They're not?

GREENSLADE: Of course not. I'm a huge fan of the show by the way.

MILLIGAN: So's everyone. That's the trouble. It was never meant to be a raving success. It was meant to be a cult. With me the biggest cult of them all.

GREENSLADE: Haven't you heard? Obscurity doesn't pay.

MILLIGAN: I know. I had a career in it for thirty five years. (*Beat.*) Am I mad, doctor?

GREENSLADE: Ah, but what is 'madness'?

MILLIGAN: You don't know? Am I in big trouble. (*Suspicious.*) You look like Wal Greenslade by the way.

GREENSLADE: The announcer from the Goon Show?

MILLIGAN: Yes.

GREENSLADE: I'm afraid I've never seen him. (*Smiles.*) My radio gets a rather poor picture.

MILLIGAN: A shrink with a crappy sense of humour? It's going to be a long breakdown.

*The sound of knocking on the door left.*

Are you going to get that?

GREENSLADE: Get what?

MILLIGAN: Can't you hear the knocking?

GREENSLADE: Knocking? No.

MILLIGAN: I know they're not there.

GREENSLADE: Who?

MILLIGAN: Them. They were here yesterday too.

GREENSLADE: You were deranged all yesterday.

MILLIGAN: Because they were here. Even if they weren't here: technically. Are you with me?

GREENSLADE: Not specifically.

*More knocking at the door left. He shouts:*

MILLIGAN: Go away. I'm a manic depressive with suicidal tendencies; this Milligan bites.

GREENSLADE: Are you talking to me or 'them'?

MILLIGAN: Both I think.

GREENSLADE: I think you might need a sedative. I won't be a jiff. Try not to upset yourself.

MILLIGAN: Easier said than done.

*GREENSLADE exits right. More knocking on the door left.*

Swines.

*MILLIGAN gets up. He opens the door. SECOMBE stands before him grinning inanely. SECOMBE bursts into song:*

SECOMBE: (*Sings.*) 'We'll keep a welcome in the hillsides We'll keep a welcome in the dales. We'll –'

*MILLIGAN slams the door in SECOMBE's face.*

MILLIGAN: I die after that nit. Or he'll sing at my bleedin' funeral.

*Knocking comes from the door right.*

Be gone. I've just eaten hospital mince and I'm waiting to die.

*More knocking on the door right. A beat. Opens it again. SECOMBE is still singing. MILLIGAN slams it shut again.*

MILLIGAN: For Christ's sakes, leave me alone. I'm trying to have a nervous breakdown here, in the privacy of my own loony bin.

*Yet more knocking on the door right.*

I've said it before and I'll say it again: swines.

*He opens the door right. SELLERS stands in the doorway. Naked as the day he was born save for a for a Trilby perched at a jaunty angle on his head. Holding a folded copy of* The Daily Telegraph *which conveniently covers his privates. He lifts the hat politely.*

SELLERS: Sorry to bother you but would you happen to

know the name of a good tailor?

MILLIGAN: Goldberg and Stein: 34 Brick Lane. Knock three times and give them the secret password: 'shalom big-nose.'

SELLERS: Thank you and good day.

*SELLERS lifts his Trilby politely once more and swings the door shut on himself.*

MILLIGAN: You could tell he was Jewish. He was reading *The Daily Telegraph.*

*MILLIGAN gets back into bed.*

Talking to yourself is the first sign of madness, you know. (*2nd voice.*) I thought that was the drooling. (*1st voice.*) No, sometimes you can drool and not be insane at all. (*2nd voice.*) Do you come here often? (*1st voice.*) Not as often as I'd like. (*2nd voice.*) You're never alone with a split personality.

*GREENSLADE re-enters carrying a huge hyperdermic syringe through the door right.*

GREENSLADE: Here we are.

MILLIGAN: Where are you going to put that?

GREENSLADE: Guess.

MILLIGAN: Can things get any worse?

GREENSLADE: Turn over please.

*MILLIGAN turns over on the bed. GREENSLADE pulls down MILLIGAN's trousers.*

MILLIGAN: If you find the crew of the *Marie Celeste* up there be sure to let me know. (*Beat.*) This is no way to treat a war veteran.

GREENSLADE: You were in the war?

MILLIGAN: Yes. I was called up. Despite my constant and

brilliant virginity.

GREENSLADE: (*Laughs.*) You were a virgin when you joined up?

MILLIGAN: Only when it came to shooting strangers. (*Beat.*) I was sent to Africa.

GREENSLADE: Ah, we have a Desert Rat in our midst.

MILLIGAN: Not me. I was a desert hamster. Cowardly? I shat myself all the way.

GREENSLADE: You must have fought Rommel.

MILLIGAN: (*Nods.*) With only 47,000 other pigeon chested cowards I attacked him single-handed. (*Beat.*) He was the 'good' German. At least according to popular myth. If only our casualties had known how good he was. They'd have died without screaming.

GREENSLADE: Deep breath. This might sting a little.

*GREENSLADE injects MILLIGAN in the arse. MILLIGAN yells in pain.*

There. That didn't hurt did it?

*MILLIGAN pulls up his trousers and turns over.*

MILLIGAN: Frankly? Yes. Being shot at in North Africa didn't hurt that much. (*Beat.*) I met Harry there.

GREENSLADE: Harry?

MILLIGAN: Secombe. The singing barrage balloon. I was minding my own business, trying to shell Germans, when my artillery piece came loose and fell off a cliff, backwards. It flew over Secombe's truck. I put my head round the flap: 'Anyone seen my gun?' I said. 'What colour?' he said. Quick as a flash. I've been trying to shake the berk off ever since.

GREENSLADE: Try and be quiet now. The sedative should kick in soon.

MILLIGAN: Sorry. I've always talked too much, doctor. My parents moved to Australia to get away from the sound of my voice. I'd move to Australia myself but what the fuck is a 'billabong'?

GREENSLADE: I wouldn't have thought you'd want to leave England. Being so successful.

MILLIGAN: Yeah, look at me: writing in crayon, getting blanket baths from sadists and one step away from a lobotomy – Mr Success.

GREENSLADE: Chin up. We'll have you hunky dory in no time. Try and get some rest. It's a powerful sedative. You should sleep for quite some time.

*There comes the sound of a busy pub: Grafton's. MILLIGAN looks up at the noise:*

MILLIGAN: Don't look now, doctor, but I feel a flashback coming on:

*SELLERS and SECOMBE enter.*

(*Manic.*) Ever get a feeling of *déjà vu*? (*Beat.*) Ever get a feeling of *déjà vu*? (*Beat.*) Ever get a feeling of *déjà vu*? (*Beat.*) Ever –

*MILLIGAN slumps into a deep sleep. GREENSLADE crosses to the microphone. Speaks to audience:*

GREENSLADE: Grafton's public house, Victoria. Sometime in 1949.

*GREENSLADE exits. The noise from the pub is heard under:*

SECOMBE: This is it: Jimmy Grafton's.

SELLERS: (*Richard Dimbleby voice.*) Stepping over the yokel in the doorway, grovelling in his own rancid filth, we visit a traditional British 'pub'. Where the locals guzzle bitter like pigs from a trough. Proving England is still very much a Third World country and proud of it.

SECOMBE: (*Laughs.*) All the Windmill boys drink in here:

you'll love it.

SELLERS: Harry – it's a dump.

SECOMBE: Your trouble is you don't like pubs.

SELLERS: Your trouble is you like everything.

SECOMBE: On behalf of my parents: I apologise.

SELLERS: How did the tour go?

SECOMBE: The notorious and highly original Secombe shaving act went down a storm in all parts. 'Cept for Bolton where I got paid off. Shaved in total silence to a full house. (*Giggles.*) Can't win 'em all.

SELLERS: So where's this 'Spike' character?

SECOMBE: The Count of Monte Catford? He'll not be up yet. It's only two in the afternoon.

SELLERS: He lives here?

SECOMBE: In the attic. Next to where they keep Grafton's pet monkey. They serve him scraps of dog meat and chain him to the wall.

SELLERS: You mean Milligan?

SECOMBE: (*Giggles.*) Of course. They're writing together.

SELLERS: Him and the monkey? It'll never work. They'll notice the typing errors.

SECOMBE: No, fool, him and Grafton, for Derek Roy.

SELLERS: The unfunniest comedian north of the equator.

SECOMBE: What pisses me off is there's good comedy performers out there who aren't getting a sniff of radio. It's a closed shop, boy. The old guard are giving nothing away.

SELLERS: (*Mock bravado.*) Then we must take to the barricades. As soon as this pub closes the revolution starts!

SECOMBE: It's that or end up starving, boy!

SELLERS: (*Willium voice.*) Makes you wonder why we fought the bleedin' war.

SECOMBE: You weren't in the war, Pete. You were in a Gang Show. You lucky sod.

SELLERS: (*Bloodnok voice.*) How dare you. I was a Major: Major Bollocks. I was cashiered from the regiment when they found me in bed with Herman Goering. Those narrow-minded fools. Didn't they realise? In between the bottom sex I was pumping him for information.

*SECOMBE does a stiff military salute:*

SECOMBE: Major Bollocks: I salute you.

SELLERS: And so you should.

*MILLIGAN enters the scene. SECOMBE notices.*

SECOMBE: Stone me: it's Ben Gunn.

SELLERS: (*Aside.*) Far be it for me to be the voice of reason but – why's he wearing pyjamas?

SECOMBE: He's pawned his demob suit again. (*Beat.*) Hello, Spike.

MILLIGAN: Here he blows. It's Moby Secombe. Still a danger to shipping?

SECOMBE: But of course.

MILLIGAN: When did you get back?

SECOMBE: Last night.

MILLIGAN: Why didn't you come in?

SECOMBE: I thought I'd actually spend some time with my wife. I'm old fashioned that way. This is the fellow I was telling you about –

MILLIGAN: The one from the Clap Clinic?

SECOMBE: No, arse, the comic: Sellers. From *Ray's-A-Laugh.*

SELLERS: I do the odd voice.

SECOMBE: You do a whole city, boy. I thought there was eight of you.

SELLERS: There is. My mother's Jewish. She won't stop feeding me.

SECOMBE: I met Pete when he played the Windmill.

MILLIGAN: One of the chosen few, eh?

SELLERS: Jealous?

MILLIGAN: Too bloody right. They turned me down.

SELLERS: You didn't miss much. Every night was pervert night.

SECOMBE: Right. Who needs to play the Windmill, eh?

MILLIGAN: You did.

SECOMBE: Not anymore. Onwards and upwards. That's what I say. No more strippers for Secombe. (*Giggles.*) I took one home when I left but the wife made me take it back.

MILLIGAN: (*To Sellers.*) What's your act then?

SELLERS: (*Smug.*) Newsreel skits, impressions, that kind of thing, it goes rather well.

MILLIGAN: Been performing long?

SELLERS: Only since birth. My mother had a music-hall turn. We played every dump in England. The smell of greasepaint still makes me throw up. Forgive me if I don't go on. I'm beginning to bore myself.

MILLIGAN: And the rest of us.

*An awkward, slightly hostile pause. SECOMBE glances worried from one to another.*

SELLERS: Well, I suppose I should get the drinks in. Beer alright for you?

MILLIGAN: Naturally.

SELLERS: I'm a vodka and lime man myself.

MILLIGAN: Do you get a big girl's blouse with that?

*SELLERS stares straight through him.*

SELLERS: Mmm. Very good. Won't be a jiff.

*SELLERS exits. SECOMBE anxious:*

SECOMBE: So what do you think? I was thinking we could try something. Him and Bentine, you and me, you know –

MILLIGAN: It'll be a cold day in hell before I work with that bastard.

*The lights change.*

*Music: a feverish version of 'The Peanut Vendor Song'.*

*The lights rise on a Goon Show mid-progress: MILLIGAN, SELLERS, SECOMBE and GREENSLADE stand before their microphones. Scripts in hand.*

*The music fades.*

GREENSLADE: 'A Llama Called Burt: Part III'. Thus young Seagoon sailed the piranha-crazed Amazon towards the lost city of El Dorado; in a canoe cobbled together from cement, string and wishful thinking. Little realising a fiendish stowaway was aboard.

SELLERS: (*Grytpype-Thynne voice.*) Excuse me, aren't you Neddie Seagoon? Or am I mistaking you for the beached whale that can yodel like Mario Lanza?

SECOMBE: My God – Captain Grytpype-Thynne!

SELLERS: (*Grytpype-Thynne voice.*) Please don't say that name out loud.

SECOMBE: Why not?

SELLERS: (*Grytpype-Thynne voice.*) Some of my creditors have very good hearing.

SECOMBE: I heard you were doing ten years in Brixton nick for repeatedly selling Buckingham Palace to gullible American tourists.

SELLERS: (*Grytpype-Thynne voice.*) How was I to know they'd dismantle it and ship it all the way to Nebraska?

SECOMBE: How did you get out of jail?

SELLERS: (*Grytpype-Thynne voice* .) There's not a prison built can hold me!

SECOMBE: You escaped?

SELLERS: (*Grytpype-Thynne voice.*) After serving the full ten years? Of course. But to the issue at hand: I want to buy your Aztec gold-mine, Neddie. I'm prepared to offer you a colostomy bag (hardly used), a second hand IOU for one thousand forged herring and all the Hungarian goulash you can gargle.

SECOMBE: Never!

SELLERS: (*Grytpype-Thynne voice.*) Then you've left me no choice. I'm forced into using an old Comanche Indian trick.

SECOMBE: What's that?

SELLERS: (*Grytpype-Thynne voice.*) Cruelty. I have here a copy of the document on which you claimed your gold-mine.

SECOMBE: A legally binding tract: you Grammar School twister.

SELLERS: (*Grytpype-Thynne voice.*) I'm afraid not, young Neddie. In the haste to sign your name you left out a crucial 'd'.

SECOMBE: I spelt my name wrong? It cannot be. I used to have duxluxia but I'm all wrote now.

GREENSLADE: Please don't groan, dear listeners. You might just wake this audience.

SELLERS: (*Grytpype-Thynne voice.*) The claim is invalid, Seagoon. I claim your gold-mine as my own: lock, stock and midget.

MILLIGAN: (*Eccles voice.*) Who are you calling a midget? I'm not a midget. I'm just crouching.

SELLERS: (*Grytpype-Thynne voice.*) What are you doing in this canoe? There's only room for me and three of him. Have you got a swimming certificate?

MILLIGAN: (*Eccles voice.*) No.

SELLERS: (*Grytpype-Thynne voice.*) Thank God for that:

MILLIGAN: (*Eccles voice.*) Aaaaaaaaahhh!

*FX: a huge splash.*

(*Little Jim voice.*) He's fallen in the water.

SECOMBE: (*Shouts.*) You pushed him overboard!

SELLERS: (*Grytpype-Thynne voice.*) Yes, but drowning will improve his personality.

SECOMBE: Has anyone got a light buoy?

*FX: enthusiastic water splurging.*

MILLIGAN: (*Eccles voice.*) This is my first bath since VE Night. Who's hogging the rubber ducky?

*FX: the mating bellow of a sexually frustrated hippopotamus.*

SECOMBE: Eccles! What are you doing with that boss-eyed and emotionally aroused hippopotamus?

MILLIGAN: (*Eccles voice.*) I think it's the mambo. And she's taking the lead. Who's going to argue with a boss-eyed and emotionally aroused hippopotamus?

SECOMBE: If that's not a broad hint for a musical interlude nothing is.

GREENSLADE: Take it away: Ray Ellington and his four piece trio.

*Music: a fast and hypnotic version of: 'Blame It On The Mambo'.*

*The lights change.*

*They rise on MILLIGAN sitting up in bed. GREENSLADE sits at the nurse's desk. Taking notes. Once more in a doctor's white coat. The music fades.*

You were born in India?

MILLIGAN: (*Nods.*) Poona. Naked save for a pith helmet and a sneer.

GREENSLADE: That must have been – exotic.

MILLIGAN: It was magical. (*Beat.*) It was – is – a beautiful country.

GREENSLADE: Yet the locals were so pleased when we left.

MILLIGAN: (*Nods.*) They even put out flags: the ungrateful bastards. Everyone moans about the British Raj but we gave India three great things: the railways, the Bible and herpes. You can get shot of the first two but the third one always comes bouncing back.

GREENSLADE: Do you miss it?

MILLIGAN: What? Herpes?

GREENSLADE: (*Sighs.*) India.

MILLIGAN: Of course. You can blame me? I work in Shepherd's Bush. Save for Queens Park Rangers and the wholesale prostitution it's a cultural desert.

GREENSLADE: Yet you never go back.

MILLIGAN: No. It's not the place I knew. (*Beat.*) What do you get when you cross India with Pakistan? War. (*Beat.*) I miss my childhood not the country.

GREENSLADE: So why did your parents move to Catford?

MILLIGAN: To get a better view of the Taj Mahal.

GREENSLADE: And really?

MILLIGAN: My Dad was a sergeant major. The army sacked him for gross and glaring competence. We got back to England just in time for the Depression. How we laughed.

GREENSLADE: I remember it well. Who could forget?

MILLIGAN: It was harder for us. We thought we were Anglo-Indian you see, 'the master race', but we were only working class.

GREENSLADE: How old were you?

MILLIGAN: Fifteen. I never went to school. Not here. We couldn't afford it. I got a job in a cigarette factory. Where I was unjustly accused of stealing.

GREENSLADE: Why was that?

MILLIGAN: Because the over-suspicious sods found two thousand fags hidden about my person come clocking out time. I stole them 'cause I was saving for a trumpet. I never wanted to be a comedian. I wanted to be a musician. I only became a comedian to avoid starvation. With skill, application and dedication to my craft I ended up – starving. Sharing a room above a pub with a monkey. But the rent was peanuts. It had to be. The monkey was the landlord.

GREENSLADE: Do you always use jokes to deflect pain?

MILLIGAN: Only for forty years.

GREENSLADE: That's not very healthy.

MILLIGAN: Isn't it? I was signing on in 1935. Me and the rest of the world. I was in the dole queue at Lewisham Labour Exchange when the man in front of me keeled over and died. So the bloke behind me said: 'someone must have offered him a bleeding job.' I laughed. What else could I do? That man died of poverty and hunger. Yet they were still eating caviar at the Ritz. It's joke or let the bitterness kill you.

GREENSLADE: Did you ever earn a living as a musician?

MILLIGAN: Seldom if never. I was going back to it after the war: music. But meeting Sellers, Secombe and Bentine ended all that; the Mummy's boy, the singing leek and the Peruvian from Watford. I became a Goon instead. He sobbed. (*Beat.*) Were you in the war?

GREENSLADE: (*Shakes head.*) Flat feet. Served in the Home Guard. Guarding Ealing Broadway Station against the Teutonic hordes.

MILLIGAN: I ironed my feet but they still enlisted me.

GREENSLADE: Did you resent fighting?

MILLIGAN: Not as much as I resent these stupid bloody questions.

GREENSLADE: (*Looks at watch.*) Well, it's lunch-time. We'll stop there.

MILLIGAN: Is it mince, mince or mince?

GREENSLADE: (*Walks to door.*) Try and rest. We'll talk later.

MILLIGAN: That'll be a thrill for all concerned.

*GREENSLADE exits. A long beat. Then:*

You can come out now. He's gone.

*Enter SELLERS through the door right on his knees and dressed as a leprechaun. When he speaks it is in an absurd Irish accent.*

What kept you?

SELLERS: Hello there!

MILLIGAN: What are you?

SELLERS: Me? I'm a leprechaun. That's a pixie with a shovel.

MILLIGAN: How are things in Glocca Morra?

SELLERS: Fucking awful.

MILLIGAN: To what do I owe this honour?

SELLERS: I'm your lucky sprite. Every Irishman has one.

MILLIGAN: My father's Irish but my mother's English. Every year, on the anniversary of the Battle of the Boyne, they beat the living shit out of each other.

SELLERS: You're half English but only from the waist down. The part that's all bollocks.

MILLIGAN: What are you doing in a loony bin?

SELLERS: I could ask you the same question.

MILLIGAN: Drooling mainly. My father, ever the romantic, once said I was a direct descendant of the Kings Of Connaught. What end of kings is this?

SELLERS: Well – I'm here to bring you luck.

MILLIGAN: I don't think I'm very lucky at the moment.

SELLERS: Have you wished upon a shamrock?

MILLIGAN: Does that help?

SELLERS: Not at all. Shamrocks? Feckin' useless.

*Enter SECOMBE, through the door left, dressed as leprechaun and on his knees. He also speaks in an absurd Irish accent.*

SECOMBE: Hello there!

MILLIGAN: You're multiplying like rabbits.

SECOMBE: We're Catholics. We always breed like rabbits. (*Sings.*) 'We got music, we got rhythm, we got naughty bits, who could ask for anything more?'

MILLIGAN: I'm a Catholic atheist.

SECOMBE: Do you go to confession?

MILLIGAN: Yes, but I take a whoopee cushion with me.

SECOMBE: You've been in England too long. They're a terrible people the English: all bus-queues and buggery.

MILLIGAN: I fought for England.

SELLERS: Not against the poor soddin' Irish I hope?

MILLIGAN: In World War II. You must remember it: it was the only war Vera Lynn did the soundtrack too.

SELLERS: Ah, we didn't have a World War II in Ireland, Milligan. We just had an 'emergency.'

MILLIGAN: What was the emergency?

SELLERS: We ran out of Guinness.

MILLIGAN: Aren't you just racial stereotypes masquerading as wacky dwarves?

SECOMBE: To be sure we are. And top of the morning for mentioning it. We'll be gnawing on a potato any minute now. But aren't we just critters from your imagination, Milligan? Not here at all, at all.

MILLIGAN: True. The Home Office says I have to re-apply for citizenship, you see. As I was born outside of the United Kingdom. Despite the fact I fought a war for them for five long years. Anyway, to cut a dull story short, I'm thinking of applying for an Irish passport. Which is why I'm seeing you I suppose.

SECOMBE: Ah, we're awful short of people, Milligan. You'd be welcome. They keep pissing off to America. Even since that Kennedy fellow became president they think any Irishman can. The poor, deluded bastards.

SELLERS: Mind you, you'll have to explain what you were doing in the British bleedin' Army. You-redcoat-you.

MILLIGAN: I applied for the Irish Navy but the dingy was full.

SELLERS: Ah, a sneer at the paddies again. But what did the English ever do for you, Milligan? Save treat you like dole fodder or cannon fodder?

MILLIGAN: They made a lovely cup of tea.

SELLERS: You don't know what you are, Milligan: neither Irish nor Indian nor English. No wonder you're sick.

SECOMBE: 'A man without a country is a man without a soul.'

MILLIGAN: Who said that?

SECOMBE: I did – you deaf sod.

MILLIGAN: Can you give me some luck? I'm in need of some – fast.

SECOMBE: Of course we can. What with Cromwell.

SELLERS: The potato famine.

SECOMBE: The civil war.

SELLERS: The Black & Tans.

SECOMBE: The rain.

SELLERS: And three hundred years of oppression.

BOTH: Haven't the Irish been blessed to death with luck?

MILLIGAN: (*Laughs.*) Did you hear about the Irish mosquito? It caught malaria.

SELLERS: (*Sour.*) Why are Irish jokes so simple? So the stupid bleedin' English can understand 'em.

*Enter GREENSLADE on his knees and dressed as a leprechaun but wearing a Jewish skullcap. He speaks in an East End Jewish accent.*

GREENSLADE: Shalom there! Can any of you fellows direct me to the Yiddish goblin convention?

SELLERS: By Jeezus! It's Benny O'Cohen!

MILLIGAN: A Jewish leprechaun? Now I've seen everything.

GREENSLADE: So I'm Jewish-Irish. I go to confession but I take a lawyer with me.

MILLIGAN: That joke was old when Max Bygraves started telling it – in 1847.

GREENSLADE: Oi vey! At these prices he wants originality? What a Meshughe!

MILLIGAN: My God: it's another racially insulting stereotype.

GREENSLADE: Who's circumcised? Me or you?

MILLIGAN: I didn't want to be circumcised. I was walking through Tel Aviv when I was attacked by a deranged rabbi with a blunt penknife.

GREENSLADE: So that's why you walk like a Shikseh. But don't worry: you're still one of us.

MILLIGAN: I am? I thought I was English.

SECOMBE: Irish.

SELLERS: (*Indian accent.*) Indian. It's so confusing.

GREENSLADE: You're descended from Adam and Eve aren't you? We're all the lost tribe of Israel.

MILLIGAN: And still Lew Grade won't book me.

SELLERS: (*Looks off.*) Wait a minute: there's a rainbow over Neasden. That pot of gold at the rainbow's end has my name written on it. Last one to a shovel is a big girl's Protestant.

*SELLERS exits on his knees. SECOMBE give chase.*

SECOMBE: (*As he exits.*) Come back here you mercenary midget. Don't leave without me. If they see a lone leprechaun in Neasden they'll eat it to be sure – in a kebab.

*SECOMBE exits after SELLERS. GREENSLADE remains.*

GREENSLADE: What's the matter? Don't you like money? Why are you sitting here k'vetshing? You should be busy writing those God awful scripts the Goyim find so funny. Never mind the quality: feel the cheque.

MILLIGAN: I can't.

GREENSLADE: Why not?

MILLIGAN: I keep getting interrupted by Jewish leprechauns.

GREENSLADE: You've an excuse for everything you, haven't you, boy?

MILLIGAN: I care too much for my scripts to churn them out.

GREENSLADE: It's just gibberish, man.

MILLIGAN: Yes, but it's my gibberish. There'll never be gibberish like it again.

GREENSLADE: Oi! What a Nudnick! I'm off. Up the 29 counties!

MILLIGAN: I thought it was 32 counties?

GREENSLADE: To you: 27 counties! A nation once again? I can get it for you wholesale!

*GREENSLADE exits. A silence. He sighs.*

MILLIGAN: They're right: Irish, English and Indian? I sound like a racist joke. (*Depressed.*) Maybe that's all I am: a racist joke.

*Then there comes the sound of a busy public house. MILLIGAN looks up:*

Not another flashback? Oh shit. (*Shouts.*) Go away. I don't want to drive down Memory Lane anymore. I'm out of bloody petrol. This car's kaput, ready for the knackers yard, can't you leave me be?

*SELLERS enters.*

Oh God: here we again – *déjà* fucking *vu.*

SELLERS: Don't swear, Spike. Someone's mother might be in.

MILLIGAN: Sorry. (*Frowns.*) I'm apologising to a flashback?

*Enter SECOMBE. The noise of the pub plays below:*

SELLERS: (*Larry Olivier impression.*) 'Angels and ministers of grace defend us. Be thou spirit of health or goblin damn'd'?

SECOMBE: The melancholy Dane?

SELLERS: (*Larry Olivier impression.*) But of course.

SECOMBE: It must be marvellous to be educated. He sneered.

SELLERS: Don't play the peasant card, Harry. You're the most well read man I know.

SECOMBE: (*Winks.*) Keep it under your hat – I'm fooling them.

SELLERS: Why did we have to meet here?

SECOMBE: Why not meet here?

SELLERS: I don't like pubs.

SECOMBE: You don't like anything.

SELLERS: (*Beat.*) Well –

SECOMBE: Was that an awkward conversational turn?

SELLERS: Yes. (*Beat.*) Have you spoken to Milligan?

SECOMBE: He's not doing it.

SELLERS: He's got to.

SECOMBE: You're problem is you think the world revolves around you.

SELLERS: (*Mock surprise.*) It doesn't?

SECOMBE: No.

SELLERS: So I want to be the biggest.

SECOMBE: What? Twerp?

SELLERS: Comic actor of my generation. Is that a crime?

SECOMBE: Where's that leave the Goons?

SELLERS: It's an obsession, a magnificent obsession; I'll cross oceans to keep doing it.

SECOMBE: I want to carry on as much as you do but your obsession is sending Milligan barmy.

SELLERS: (*Larry Olivier voice.*) Methinks he doth protest too much.

SECOMBE: One of these days you'll do a voice and you'll get stuck with it.

SELLERS: We've got to get him to write another series.

SECOMBE: Even if it kills him?

SELLERS: They're just words.

SECOMBE: They're more than that to Milligan. They're driving him to despair.

SELLERS: (*Laughs.*) I know all about despair: my Dad's a Yorkshireman.

SECOMBE: It's not a joke, Pete. We can't go on and on at him.

SELLERS: Really? I can.

SECOMBE: Then shame on you.

SELLERS: You're not my conscience, Harry.

SECOMBE: Yes I am. I always bloody am. Time you had one of your own, boy.

*A silence. SELLERS looks around him.*

SELLERS: I do loathe pubs you know.

SECOMBE: Only 'cause you have to mingle with the unwashed hordes. (*Beat.*) Does the Great Sellers want a drink?

SELLERS: (*Larry Olivier voice.*) When in Rome.

SECOMBE: If Sir Larry isn't gone by the time I get back I'm kicking his head in.

*SECOMBE exits. In perfect Larry Olivier voice, half-seriously we suspect, he transforms himself into the hunchbacked Richard III and recites:*

SELLERS: 'But I – that am not shap'd for sportive tricks
Nor made to court an amorous looking-glass
I – that am rudely stamp'd, and want love's majesty
To strut before a wanton ambling nymph –
I – that am curtail'd of this fair proportion,
Cheated of feature by dissembling nature,
Deform'd, unfinish'd, sent before my time
Into this breathing world scarce half made up,

And that so lamely and unfashionable
That dogs bark at me as I halt by them –
Why, I, in this weak piping time of peace,
Have no delight to pass away the time,
Unless to spy my shadow in the sun
And descant of my own deformity.'

*He turns and stares at MILLIGAN. MILLIGAN stares back. MILLIGAN begins to applaud. Slow-hand and with relentless irony. SELLERS bows mockingly.*

MILLIGAN: How come you never impersonate me?

SELLERS: I can't do you, Spike.

MILLIGAN: What a coincidence: neither can I.

SELLERS: (*Charlady voice.*) I know you think I don't care, boyo. But I expect I'll look back on working with you as the best days of my life.

MILLIGAN: Then why can't you say it in your normal voice?

SELLERS: I can't do me either, Spike. I haven't got a 'me'. I had it surgically removed.

MILLIGAN: Excuses, excuses.

SELLERS: (*Bleak.*) If only they were.

*SELLERS exits. MILLIGAN calls after him:*

MILLIGAN: You put the git in 'Highgit'.

*MILLIGAN glances around, gets up and approaches typewriter, sits at nurse's desk.*

Screw these mirages. Time to write. I'll show those BBC tosspots. The British Bastard Corporation? A conglomerate of crap. Postmen with cameras. Jobsworths. Desk pilots. Office wallahs. Zombies of officialdom. Zealots of tedium. Vampires of talent. Blood sucking bureaucrats. Corpses in suits. Fat arsed fools. Oxbridge arse-wipes. Time serving lick-spittles who treat you like a leper if you dream of greater things than their dreary, pen pushing wank. Liars. Cowards. Train-spotters. Thieves. Worst of all? Those bastards don't dance. Am I biting the hand that feeds? With sadistic bleedin' glee.

*A long silence. He stares at the typewriter and the paper in it.*

Stalling. Milligan's stalling. Writer's block. Isn't it bloody marvellous? (*Desperate.*) Write something. In the name of God: write something. You need to write something. You can't afford not to. There's no pension scheme for failed comedians. Time for the comic talent to flow like silver. But what if that's gone awol with my marbles? Great. (*Desperate.*) SNAFU – situation normal, all fucked up.

*A silence. Then GREENSLADE enters. In a head scarf and woman's coat. He should play the following scene gently without comic inflection. He sings as he enters:*

GREENSLADE: (*Sings.*) When Irish eyes are smiling
Sure 'tis like a morn in Spring
With the lilt of Irish laughter
You can hear the angels sing.

MILLIGAN: What fresh hell is this?

GREENSLADE: Hello love.

MILLIGAN: Who are you?

GREENSLADE: Your wife.

MILLIGAN: I didn't think we were talking.

GREENSLADE: We're not.

MILLIGAN: Then why are my lips moving?

GREENSLADE: I've come to tell you something.

MILLIGAN: That I'm mad? It's common knowledge. It's

even made the pages of *Titbits*.

GREENSLADE: I'm leaving you.

MILLIGAN: You've just got here.

GREENSLADE: I've met someone. A man.

MILLIGAN: At a time like this?

GREENSLADE: I've been alone too long.

MILLIGAN: You weren't alone: you had me.

GREENSLADE: I never had you, Spike. Your obsession had you. Your writing obsession. It took over your life. I always came second. Sometimes third.

MILLIGAN: Third?

GREENSLADE: Oh, I knew about your little affairs, Spike. Wives always do.

MILLIGAN: They didn't mean anything.

GREENSLADE: Only to me, Spike, only to me. (*Beat.*) He wants me to move in with him.

MILLIGAN: What about the kids?

GREENSLADE: I'm taking them with me.

MILLIGAN: You can't.

GREENSLADE: Watch me.

MILLIGAN: But they're my life.

GREENSLADE: They're not mine?

MILLIGAN: What'll I be without my children? I'm nothing without my children. I can make them believe there's fairies at the bottom of my garden. No, it's the reverse. They make me believe.

GREENSLADE: There's no such things as fairies at the bottom of the garden, Spike. There never was.

MILLIGAN: And you wonder why I found it so hard to love you?

*A silence.*

Who is he? Do I know him?

GREENSLADE: He's a Covent Garden porter.

MILLIGAN: How did he woo you? With thirty crappy verses of *Wouldn't It Be Lovely*?

GREENSLADE: Don't get bitter, Spike.

MILLIGAN: I am bitter. How quickly they forget.

GREENSLADE: Not always. I'll miss the laughs we had.

MILLIGAN: What laughs? I suffered from depression the whole of our marriage.

GREENSLADE: No better then?

MILLIGAN: Worse. Much worse.

GREENSLADE: What do the doctors say?

MILLIGAN: There's no known cure. But they've decided to rally round and keep charging me anyway.

GREENSLADE: It was never easy.

MILLIGAN: What?

GREENSLADE: Being married to someone who finds it so difficult to live. I got guilty, you see.

MILLIGAN: Guilty?

GREENSLADE: That I should have helped in some way. But there's no help to give is there? You can only stand by and wonder why your husband locks himself away for days at a time.

MILLIGAN: The isolation helped. Sometimes.

GREENSLADE: People think of you as a funny man but you've done a thousand times more suffering than laughing.

MILLIGAN: Yes.

GREENSLADE: I've never known that a human being could be in despair so completely. All I could ever offer was love. But that was never enough, was it?

MILLIGAN: I'm – sorry.

GREENSLADE: It's not your fault. My problem is: I thought it was mine.

MILLIGAN: I don't know what to say. I haven't got the words. I'm a writer: I'm supposed to have the words. But – I don't. Not for this.

GREENSLADE: Be strong. Don't you remember? You're descended from the Kings of Connaught.

*GREENSLADE starts to back towards the door.*

MILLIGAN: (*Desperate.*) But they were mad bastards too.

GREENSLADE: (*At the doorway.*) Be happy, Spike.

MILLIGAN: (*Almost tearful.*) I can't. I don't know how.

*GREENSLADE sings softly:*

GREENSLADE: (*Sings.*) When Irish hearts are happy
All the world seems bright and gay
But when Irish eyes are smiling
Sure they steal your heart away.

*GREENSLADE exits.*

MILLIGAN: (*Calls after him.*) Don't go. Let's talk about this. (*Beat.*) I'll fight for the kids – I swear. I refuse to be a sad bastard weekend Dad riding sad bastard Sunday trains. It'll get ugly. (*To himself.*) As if it hasn't already. (*Calls.*) You proposed to me. I never proposed to you. June? June? (*Confused.*) Wal? Greenslade? Was that you or her? Doc? (*Almost in wonder.*) I can't tell the difference between any of them anymore.

*A long silence. Then SECOMBE enters whistling cheerfully through the door right.*

SECOMBE: Is this the cage where they keep the loony bird?

MILLIGAN: (*Dubious.*) Harry?

SECOMBE: Who else would I be?

MILLIGAN: Eh – I keep seeing things.

SECOMBE: Like what?

MILLIGAN: You and Sellers. Oh, and Greenslade. Sometimes you're naked, sometimes you're dressed like women.

SECOMBE: (*Laughs.*) Calling Doctor Freud!

MILLIGAN: It's not funny:

SECOMBE: If I was a mirage: could I do this?

*SECOMBE blows a huge raspberry.*

MILLIGAN: (*Relieved.*) Thank God. But do you always have to do the raspberry?

SECOMBE: To you it's just a raspberry: to me it's a career move, mate.

MILLIGAN: What are you doing here?

SECOMBE: Visiting you, you miserable git.

MILLIGAN: You know I like you, Harry, but do me a favour and piss off.

SECOMBE: I'd say 'make me' but as I'm sixteen stone of pure blubber and you're three stone of bulimic goal-post it wouldn't be a fair fight.

MILLIGAN: You're not going away are you?

SECOMBE: Not until they sound the dinner gong.

MILLIGAN: I wouldn't bother. It's mince again. Third

time this week. This place has its own abattoir.

*SECOMBE glances at the typewriter on the nurse's desk.*

SECOMBE: (*Reading paper in typewriter.*) So – doing much writing?

MILLIGAN: No. Well – just some poems.

SECOMBE: (*Reads.*) 'On the Ning Nang Nong where the cows go bong.' (*Beat.*) Poems won't get the baby fed.

MILLIGAN: Whose baby?

SECOMBE: Anybody's baby.

MILLIGAN: I know why you're here.

SECOMBE: You do?

MILLIGAN: Do I look like an idiot?

SECOMBE: I refuse to answer that on the grounds it will incriminate you.

MILLIGAN: I can't write them, Harry.

SECOMBE: Just one more series, Spike. You know it makes sense.

MILLIGAN: It makes no sense to me.

SECOMBE: I miss doing it, boy. Sundays just aren't the same.

MILLIGAN: So get a hobby, fly a kite.

SECOMBE: I miss you too.

MILLIGAN: Is this emotional blackmail?

SECOMBE: To be frank? Yes. Anyway, I need the money.

MILLIGAN: Money can't buy you happiness.

SECOMBE: (*Laughs.*) No, but it allows you to be miserable in exotic locations.

MILLIGAN: It physically hurts me to write those bloody things. I can't do it anymore.

SECOMBE: What else would you do with your time?

MILLIGAN: I've got a packed schedule actually. As soon as you leave I'm committing suicide.

SECOMBE: How you going to do that?

MILLIGAN: Easy: inhale next to the food trolley.

SECOMBE: You won't kill yourself.

MILLIGAN: Why not?

SECOMBE: Three reasons.

MILLIGAN: What are they?

SECOMBE: Your children.

MILLIGAN: Play the pathos card, why don't you?

SECOMBE: You won't top yourself, boy. You're in this for the duration. In sickness and in health –

MILLIGAN: For poorer or poorer –

SECOMBE: (*Grins.*) Touché.

MILLIGAN: It's not funny. You and Sellers get a hundred pounds a week. Know how much I get? Twenty five.

SECOMBE: So get a better agent, pray to a bigger God.

MILLIGAN: How come Sellers get a hundred pounds a week?

SECOMBE: Because he does the best comic voices you or me have heard in our lifetimes. It's the little things, boy.

MILLIGAN: Where was Sellers when I was fighting in Italy?

SECOMBE: (*Camp voice.*) We can't all be heroes, dear.

MILLIGAN: While he was doing Gang Shows for bored

servicemen I was putting my life on the line.

SECOMBE: The way you talk it's like you fought that war alone. I hate to break it to you but there were about two hundred million other poor sods involved.

MILLIGAN: They aren't me.

SECOMBE: Hang on a minute, Monty of El Alamein. I fought the same battles as you. They shot the same bullets at me as they did as you. I took a direct hit from an 88mm and lived to tell the tale.

MILLIGAN: Only because you ate it.

SECOMBE: Don't cop out of this with fat jokes. I lived through the same hell as you, mush. How come I've stayed balanced and sane?

MILLIGAN: I don't know. I wish I knew but I don't. You're a happy saint. I'm not. Just what do you want from me?

SECOMBE: Another series.

MILLIGAN: Deserts will freeze and mountains fall into the bloody sea, Harry.

SECOMBE: (*Depressed.*) I'll take that as a no then.

*A beat. Then enter SELLERS as 'Doctor Von Krieg': a Strangelove-like therapist who speaks with a strong German accent.*

SELLERS: I'm afraid visiting hours are over, Herr?

SECOMBE: Secombe.

SELLERS: But of course: the light operatic singer.

SECOMBE: (*Goes cross eyed.*) I'm no singer and I've recorded over two hundred songs to prove it.

SELLERS: Humility? How very English.

SECOMBE: Welsh. We're good at rugby and shooting

41

Zulus. (*Giggles.*) But not at the same time.

SELLERS: (*Oblivious.*) You have to go now, Herr Semen. (*Shouts.*) I want to be alone! (*Smiles menacingly.*) With my patient naturally.

SECOMBE: Ah, well, off back to Cheam I suppose.

MILLIGAN: Don't leave me with this wanker.

SELLERS: (*Frowns.*) Is 'wanker' a bad thing?

MILLIGAN: In your case? Yes.

SECOMBE: Don't worry, Spike, you'll be up and around in no time.

MILLIGAN: Ever the bloody optimist.

SECOMBE: That's why you love me. (*To SELLERS.*) Look after him, doc.

SELLERS: But of course, huge Celtic person.

*SECOMBE exits.*

So – Herr Mulligan.

MILLIGAN: That's Milligan.

SELLERS: Whatever. You English are so – anal.

MILLIGAN: Who exactly are you?

SELLERS: I am Doctor Von Krieg. I am your new psychiatrist. (*Shouts.*) From now on there will order, discipline and sacrifice.

MILLIGAN: You sound like Hitler. Are you a Nazi or something?

SELLERS: No, like seventy million other Germans I opposed the Nazis. Very quietly. I muttered things behind their backs. Sometimes I pulled faces. They say we were the only country in World War Two without a resistance movement but that's a lie, a lie I tell you. We didn't know about those camps. We thought all those men in SS uniforms were traffic wardens. (*Pulls himself together.*) But enough about me, let's talk about you. You have the problem. I hear you're one squirrel short of a tree: nutty as a Bavarian fruitcake.

MILLIGAN: What kind of psychiatrist are you?

SELLERS: I am a strict Freudian. If you answer my questions wrongly I shall be forced to strike you repeatedly over the knuckles with a ruler. So tell me, Mr Milligan: why did you, if I can talk technically, turn into a nail-biting, bed wetting loon?

MILLIGAN: I'm a classic manic-depressive apparently. I have all the signs. The seven major symptoms of mania and hypo mania: last one to wear a tutu is a sissy.

SELLERS: Infectious mood – yes.

MILLIGAN: $E = mc^2$, Crippin had a third nipple, aliens built Ipswich.

SELLERS: Mmm. Rapid flow of ideas.

MILLIGAN: Look at me, Ma – I'm Jesus.

SELLERS: Exaggerated self-esteem. But of course.

MILLIGAN: Look at me, Ma – I'm bigger than Jesus.

SELLERS: Grandiose ideas and delusions: *ja.*

MILLIGAN: I'll show you mine if you show me yours.

SELLERS: Loss of sexual and social inhibitions: you scamp.

MILLIGAN: Piss off – quickly.

SELLERS: Of course: irritability and impatience.

MILLIGAN: (*Points at ceiling.*) Look, a kestrel.

SELLERS: Marked distractibility: *natürlich.*

MILLIGAN: Throw in pressurised speech, physical over-activity, lack of sex drive and general insomnia and you've got the whole bleeding deck.

SELLERS: *Mein Gott*: the bats are running the belfry. (*Beat.*) Tell me – were you in the war?

MILLIGAN: Yes. I was paid by my government to kill people: Germans mostly.

SELLERS: I see. (*Mutters.*) Limey bastard. (*Beat.*) Did you have a good war?

MILLIGAN: Only Rommel had that. At least according to James Mason. But I was holding my own until Italy.

SELLERS: What happened in Italy?

MILLIGAN: I volunteered for a mission, went up a mountain, got wounded, came back down a mountain. Only part of me stayed up there forever.

SELLERS: Which part?

MILLIGAN: My sanity.

SELLERS: Would you call yourself something of, what we call in Freudian circles, a whiner?

MILLIGAN: My argument is that the rest of humanity don't whine enough. If I meet another cabbie who shouts: 'cheer up mate, it might never happen' I'll kill them. World War Two happened. Korea happened. The Cold War happened. If Russia doesn't nuke us the Americans will. The world's on the brink of wholesale slaughter and I'm supposed to be chipper? And what about Auschwitz? Dachau? Buchenwald? I'm supposed to just forget them?

SELLERS: (*Shouts.*) No matter what they said at Nuremberg: I wasn't at any of those places. I'm innocent I tell you, innocent of all charges.

MILLIGAN: You're not a psychiatrist.

SELLERS: So what were all my years in medical school in Munich eh? Merely a mirage? Mmm? (*Wistful.*) Oh, to be in Munich now that Spring is here: the milkmaids, the beer kellers, the book burning – (*Frowns.*) Where was I? (*Faraway.*) Oh yes, in bed with Eva Braun. (*Shouts.*) You're supposed to suck not blow. (*Realises where he is.*) I'm sorry – I was having a flashback.

MILLIGAN: Join the bleedin' club.

SELLERS: The authorities at the hospital have come to the only conclusion possible: (*Shouts.*) you must write or be destroyed.

MILLIGAN: (*Points an accusing finger.*) I knew it – Sellers.

SELLERS: Von Krieg, I am Von Krieg. Sellers is merely the product of your desperately unhappy imagination. An imagination that would be better served writing episodes of your ever so wacky and thoroughly English Goony Shows.

MILLIGAN: Never.

SELLERS: Then I'm afraid I have to have to send for the butch Germanic women with hair in tight buns, over-sensible shoes and lesbian tendencies. They will beat you to within an inch of your life, Herr Mulligan.

MILLIGAN: Do your worst.

SELLERS: Oh, they will, Mr Mulligan. Hell hath no fury like a hairy woman scorned.

*He clicks his heels and gives the Nazi salute. He becomes aware his arm is erect. Looks self-conscious and tries to pull his arm down.*

SELLERS: *Gott-In-Himmel.* Not in front of the cretin.

MILLIGAN: (*Grabs SELLERS.*) That's it. You're Peter Sellers and I'm going to prove it.

*MILLIGAN pulls SELLERS onto the bed and they begin*

*to grapple.*

SELLERS: (*Yells.*) Unhand me, *Schweinhund.*

*MILLIGAN gets SELLERS in a hold and begins to try to undo the zipper on his trousers.*

SELLERS: What are you doing? You mentally unhinged screwball you.

MILLIGAN: Sellers is circumcised like me. Let's see your willy. If it has a foreskin you're in the clear.

SELLERS: Get off me – you quasi-homosexual nut.

MILLIGAN: Don't make it worse for yourself.

SELLERS: (*Panic.*) No-one male has seen my penis since the Russian Front. My Panzer had no bathroom. It was every man for himself.

MILLIGAN: Don't struggle. You know this makes sense.

SELLERS: Let my private parts be, you Anglo-Irish freak. And my trousers. They were a Christmas present from Goebbels I tell you.

*MILLIGAN overcomes SELLERS' resistance and manages to look inside his zipper.*

MILLIGAN: Ah – your dick has a helmet.

SELLERS: (*Shouts.*) I am a former soldier of the Wehrmacht. Of course my penis wears a helmet.

MILLIGAN: I'm sorry.

SELLERS: Germany said sorry to Israel. (*Laughs scornfully.*) Like we meant it.

MILLIGAN: (*Shouts.*) You Nazi prick.

SELLERS: Speaking of pricks: (*Scottish accent.*) get your filthy, stinking hands off mine.

MILLIGAN: (*Confused.*) You've got a Scottish accent.

SELLERS: (*Scottish accent.*) I'm Doctor Murdock. I'm from Perth. Of course I've got a Scottish bloody accent.

*GREENSLADE enters in a hurry dressed in a doctor's coat. MILLIGAN still has his hands in SELLERS' flies.*

GREENSLADE: What in the name of God are you doing? Doctor Murdock: are you alright?

SELLERS: (*Scottish accent.*) I was examining him and he just attacked me. Pinned me to the bed and opened my flies. He had the strength of ten men. I've never been so embarrassed in my life. I'm afraid I might well have to report this to the hospital authorities.

*SELLERS exits right.*

MILLIGAN: (*Dazed.*) But he was Von Krieg.

GREENSLADE: 'Krieg'? Isn't that German for war?

MILLIGAN: I suppose it is.

GREENSLADE: If you attack the staff again we'll have to place you in a strait-jacket, Mr Milligan. We'd have no alternative.

MILLIGAN: Anything but that.

GREENSLADE: I think you might need another sedative.

MILLIGAN: Make that a double.

*There comes the sound of music: Debussy's 'Clair de Lune'; MILLIGAN looks up at the sound.*

Can you hear that, doc? The music?

GREENSLADE: No.

MILLIGAN: (*Defeated.*) Didn't think so.

GREENSLADE: I won't be long.

*GREENSLADE exits.*

MILLIGAN: Is this a flashback or a flashback of a

flashback? If it is a flashback: where's the bleedin' fog?

*A snap blackout. The music gets louder and louder still. The lights rise. The stage is deserted. SELLERS enters. Listens to the classical music alone. Enter SECOMBE. He shouts above the noise:*

SECOMBE: Peter? Peter?

SELLERS: (*Flicking off music with controls.*) A little late to be calling round, Harry –

SECOMBE: It's Spike.

SELLERS: What about him?

SECOMBE: The psychiatric hospital called.

SELLERS: (*Pales.*) He's not –

SECOMBE: Worse. He's escaped. I'm joking but I've spent half the night looking for him. (*Beat.*) What are you doing listening to classical music at four o'clock in the morning?

SELLERS: I always listen to classical music at four o'clock in the morning.

SECOMBE: Doesn't Ann mind?

SELLERS: You know, I've never ever thought to ask her.

SECOMBE: If that sentence doesn't sum up the problems in your personality nothing does.

SELLERS: We can't all be saints, Harry. Some of us are made of humbler clay.

SECOMBE: Don't start the St Harry routine again or I'll slap you. Someone has to keep this ship afloat.

SELLERS: What ship?

SECOMBE: HMS Goonery. Do you think I like being the referee between you and Milligan all the bloody time? There's days I'd like to be totally unreasonable.

SELLERS: You wouldn't know how to.

SECOMBE: If that sentence doesn't sum up the problems in my personality nothing does.

SELLERS: Where have you looked?

SECOMBE: All over north London. How far can you get from Muswell Hill in your pyjamas?

SELLERS: He'll turn up – he always does.

SECOMBE: Your concern overwhelms me.

SELLERS: I'd help you look myself but I sent the Jag back to the show-room.

SECOMBE: You've just bought it.

SELLERS: I didn't like the colour.

SECOMBE: How many cars can one man have in one lifetime?

SELLERS: Is that a trick question?

SECOMBE: I knew it'd end in tears.

SELLERS: What?

SECOMBE: Encouraging Spike to move into this block. You live in each other's shadows. It's not healthy. You wonder why I piss off back to Cheam every chance I get? We all need a bolt hole. Away from the madness and each other – it keeps you sane.

SELLERS: You'll always be sane, Harry. It's your only fault.

SECOMBE: On behalf of the mentally balanced imbeciles of the world I apologise.

SELLERS: You can't blame me for Spike going gaga. There's no-one more supportive.

SECOMBE: I can't argue with the absurdity of that

statement right now. I'll go back out. Hopefully he's heading this way. June's worried sick. I was just 'round –

*MILLIGAN enters.*

SELLERS: Spike. What are you doing here?

MILLIGAN: The door was open.

SECOMBE: You're still supposed to be in the hospital, boy. You're not a well man.

MILLIGAN: Yes. I know. But I've been thinking things through and I've decided there's only one solution to the situation.

SECOMBE: What's that?

MILLIGAN: I have to kill Peter.

SELLERS: I'm sorry?

*MILLIGAN produces a small potato peeler. Clutched in his right hand.*

SECOMBE: What's that?

MILLIGAN: It's a potato peeler. I stole it from the kitchens of the hospital. Don't worry: it's clean. They'll be no infection.

SECOMBE: You're going to kill Peter with a potato peeler?

MILLIGAN: It won't take long.

SELLERS: You can't kill a man with a potato peeler. (*Beat.*) Can you?

MILLIGAN: I was trained to be an assassin by the British Army for five and a half years. I can kill anyone with anything.

SELLERS: You're not serious.

MILLIGAN: Oh, I'm quite serious. It's nothing personal.

SELLERS: There's nothing more personal than killing

someone, Spike. (*To SECOMBE.*) I think we'd better ring for the men in white coats.

MILLIGAN: I can't let you do that, Peter. I just want you to know that after I have killed you I will look after your wife and children.

SELLERS: Will you stop looking at me like that.

MILLIGAN: How am I looking?

SELLERS: As if you're going to kill me.

MILLIGAN: There's a reason for that, Peter. I am going to kill you.

SECOMBE: Give me the peeler, boy.

MILLIGAN: Harry, don't get in the way. I like you but if I have to kill you in order to kill him I will.

SECOMBE: This is madness.

MILLIGAN: That's the technical description, yes.

SELLERS: (*Yells.*) Ann? Ann? Ring the bloody hospital. Milligan's gone mad.

MILLIGAN: Will you please stand still? It'll take longer if you don't stand still.

*SECOMBE comes between them as MILLIGAN lunges at SELLERS.*

SECOMBE: Spike, let's be sensible –

MILLIGAN: Why are you always in the way?

SECOMBE: (*Angry.*) It's my job: I'm a referee to maniacs. Didn't you know?

MILLIGAN: Not now, Harry. Peter? Do you want me to stab you in the heart or the throat?

SELLERS: What kind of choice is that?

MILLIGAN: Hobson's.

SELLERS: Bollocks to Hobson.

MILLIGAN: You shouldn't use the 'b' word, Pete. You're about to meet your maker.

SELLERS: (*Distracted.*) Bollocks is swearing?

*MILLIGAN lunges at SELLERS. SECOMBE grapples with him. SELLERS joins him.*

*As SECOMBE wrestles with him MILLIGAN looks up into his face:*

MILLIGAN: (*Desperate.*) Ever get the feeling it's not your life?

*A snap blackout.*

*Music: 'We'll Meet Again' by Vera Lynn played at a deranged, Pinky & Perky speed.*

*When the lights rise MILLIGAN is in bed. Wearing a strait jacket. Staring ahead. The music fades and is replaced by the sounds of distant battle. MILLIGAN looks up at the noise and shivers. GREENSLADE enters wearing an NCO hat and carrying a Sergeant Major's baton. He yells the following:*

GREENSLADE: Get out of that bed you filthy little man. I'll give you sick note. You're a disgrace to the British Army. We'll make a man of you yet. You can't win battles with Pansy bleedin' Potters. Call those pyjamas camouflage? War never ends, Gunner Milligan. It's eternal. Peace is an abstract concept. What's the Goon Show but a war of nerves? Stand to attention when I'm talking to you, you miserable, malingering bastard.

*A beat. SECOMBE enters through the door right. Wearing a surgeon's apron and pushing a food trolley whilst brandishing a ladle.*

SECOMBE: Time for your daily dose of boiled mince, Mr Milligan. I'm Nurse Beadle. More? More? You're going to get more alright. Only this time it's not going through your mouth. I'm afraid we're going to give you a mince enema. Think that'll hurt? (*Darkly.*) Wait 'til I administer the dumplings.

*A beat. Suddenly the door left opens. SELLERS, wearing an Adolf Hitler moustache and a Nazi armband, appears dramatically in the doorway. MILLIGAN looks stunned.*

SELLERS: So we meet again, Gunner Milligan. Argentina was boring. I'm back. And I'm invading Poland. Only this time: no more Mr Nice Guy.

*FX: the sounds of war get louder still. Reaching a crescendo. As MILLIGAN begins to yell in anguish – a snap blackout.*

*End of Act One.*

# ACT TWO

*Darkness. In the darkness music. Tommy Steele sings 'Little White Bull.'*

*The lights rise on MILLIGAN. Half dozing. Still in a strait jacket. GREENSLADE – dressed as the doctor – sits at the nurse's desk reading.*

*The music fades.*

*GREENSLADE glances up at the audience:*

GREENSLADE: 1960. St. Luke's Hospital, Muswell Hill. Tommy Steele is still number one in the Hit Parade with *Little White Bull.* A nation mourns.

*He returns to his reading. MILLIGAN's eyes open.*

MILLIGAN: What's the book?

GREENSLADE: *Lady Chatterley's Lover.*

MILLIGAN: Wake me when you get to the knobbing.

GREENSLADE: If you insist.

MILLIGAN: 'The slaughter-house behind the front door'. That's what D H Lawrence used to call domesticity. He wasn't wrong was he?

GREENSLADE: Wasn't he?

MILLIGAN: Not in my house he wasn't. (*Beat.*) My father used to drink with George Orwell, you know.

GREENSLADE: Really?

MILLIGAN: While we were stationed in Rangoon. Sergeant Blair as he was then. Save for the cage on his head with the rat in it he was as normal as the next man. (*Worried.*) I think that was a literary joke. No wonder it didn't get a laugh.

GREENSLADE: Ah.

MILLIGAN: Telling jokes. What a waste of bloody life eh?

GREENSLADE: Is it?

MILLIGAN: It started as soon as the Goons began: the pressure. Over night we developed a huge following. They were doing the catch-phrases on building sites, in offices, pubs, Buckingham Palace for Christ's sakes.

GREENSLADE: (*Bluebottle voice.*) Even Her Majesty the Queeb?

MILLIGAN: Even her. It was like a long dark tunnel in the end, maintaining the success. The light got further and further away. Until all I could see was the dark.

GREENSLADE: Isn't that a definition of psychiatry? A way to help people find their light?

*A silence. In the silence SELLERS and SECOMBE (unseen by GREENSLADE) enter dressed as Morris Dancers and silently stare at MILLIGAN. SELLERS carries a rope with a noose which he dangles before him.*

MILLIGAN: Did I ever tell you about Coventry, doc?

GREENSLADE: Not that I recall.

MILLIGAN: We played it as a trio: Peter, Harry and I. The audience loathed me on sight. I was playing a trumpet solo and they began mass booing. 'You hate me, don't you?' I said.

GREENSLADE: Asking a stupid question.

MILLIGAN: Precisely. To a man and woman they responded: 'Yes.' So I said: 'I hope you all get bombed again.' Strangely enough, as most of the city was still rubble, the booing increased.

GREENSLADE: What did you do?

MILLIGAN: I jumped up and down on my trumpet in

tears and rushed to my dressing room, determined to kill myself. I had a rope, you see. I was saving it for a rainy day.

GREENSLADE: 'Saving it'?

MILLIGAN: Call me Mr Positive. Anyway Secombe and Sellers, dressed as Morris Dancers for reasons best forgotten, had to break down the door to stop me. Maybe they shouldn't have. Maybe that was the time to go. It would have saved the people who loved me an ocean of pain.

GREENSLADE: Why didn't you? Hang yourself?

MILLIGAN: I suppose Secombe talked me round. As usual. I wish I could be like Harry: sane and good and true. But you can only be yourself. Whatever that is. The wheel's in my head got broken. They'll never turn properly again.

*SELLERS and SECOMBE exit. Staring back at MILLIGAN. A silence.*

GREENSLADE: Sixty million people died in the last world war, Mr Milligan. We should never forget them. But what about the survivors? They're victims too. Who remembers them? They lived through slaughter beyond belief. Yet they're supposed to just come home and forget. As if it never happened. But what happens to the ones that can't?

MILLIGAN: What does?

GREENSLADE: (*Smiles.*) Well, actually, they often end up here.

MILLIGAN: That's a comfort.

GREENSLADE: What I mean is: you're not alone.

MILLIGAN: I'm not? You could have fooled me.

*GREENSLADE stands:*

GREENSLADE: Think about it what I've said. Try and relax in the meantime.

MILLIGAN: In a strait jacket?

GREENSLADE: I have to see Mr Montgomery in Room 9.

MILLIGAN: The bloke who thinks he's Gracie Fields?

GREENSLADE: (*Nods.*) Sings *The Biggest Aspidistra In The World* like a dream.

MILLIGAN: You should piss in his mouth for crimes against melody. I've been trying to do that to the real Gracie Fields for years.

*GREENSLADE exits. MILLIGAN stares around him bleakly; then begins to talk to himself:*

Repeat after me: I will not die here. I will not die here. I will not die here. I will see my children grow. I will see my children grow. This can't go on, Milligan. You have to free yourself. Or you'll be in this strait jacket 'til the end of your days. It's time. Time for what, Milligan? Time for the last bloody Goon Show of all.

*Closes his eyes tight shut.*

If I wish and wish and wish: I'll never go back to Catford.

*A snap blackout.*

*Music: 'Crazy Rhythm'.*

*Lights rise on a supposed Goon Show in progress: MILLIGAN, GREENSLADE, SELLERS and SECOMBE stand in front of their microphones.*

*The music fades.*

GREENSLADE: This is the BBC Home Service.

*FX: the collective blood-curdling screams of the desperate and the damned.*

Yes: to the happy laughter of Britain's municipal workforce, going about a busy day's malingering, we present the Goon Show and –

*Music: tympani roll. Held under:*

SELLERS: (*Orson Welles voice.*) Journey To The Centre Of Milligan's Brain.

*Music: a dramatic orchestra plays. Over this:*

GREENSLADE: A radio serial by Emile Zola, adapted from the novel by Jules Verne, from an original idea by Victor Hugo, based on the sonnet by William Shakespeare, developed from the film *Who Broke My Shower Curtain?* by Sir Alfred Hitchcock, stolen from the limerick on the wall of the Bexhill NAAFI by Dame Vera Splung. Episode One: Depravity.

*FX: the sound of a terrible snow-storm.*

SECOMBE: My name is Sir Edmund Seagoon Secombe. MC, MBE, TWIT. I was a brain surgeon when not busking on the Old Kent Road and I'd been recruited by the National Health Service to make the perilous journey to re-build Milligan's damaged mind. My extraordinary tale began as I journeyed through a snow storm past an unwashed neck, beyond recklessly unkempt sideburns towards Milligan's ear. Yes, to get to the brain we were going through the lug-hole, anoraks akimbo. With me my faithful Sherpa guide: Eccles. Half-man, half-moron, half in need of bath –

MILLIGAN: (*Eccles voice.*) Hello there!

SECOMBE: Eccles, what have you done with the huskies and sled?

MILLIGAN: (*Eccles voice.*) I left them behind. At the bottom of Milligan's feet.

SECOMBE: What, what, what, what? In the name of Wales why?

MILLIGAN: (*Eccles voice.*) They belonged to a man named 'mush.' You kept chasing after him to give them back.

SECOMBE: You idiot! 'Mush' is what you say to get the huskies moving.

MILLIGAN: (*Eccles voice.*) So much to learn – so little time. Wait a minute – what's that horrible great white thing over there? Is that a Yeti?

SECOMBE: No, that's dandruff. Besides mental infirmity? It's Milligan's only curse.

ECCLES: (*Eccles voice.*) There's a shampoo at Boots the chemists will clear that right up. Its only side effect is blindness.

SECOMBE: Now's not the time for an advertising break. (*Dramatic voice.*) We're going into that ear.

*Music: a manic burst of 'The Ride of the Valkyries'.*

GREENSLADE: Thus our intrepid heroes entered Milligan's ear. Into the grim abyss they plunged. Once there, using native Welsh cunning and years of thorough military training, they immediately got lost.

SECOMBE: (*Panicking tone.*) The dark, the infernal dark, I can't bear the endless dark. Pull yourself together, Seagoon. You've survived the Glasgow Empire, you can survive this. And the audience there tried to stone me to death with stale scones. All for singing *They Call The Wind Mariah.* The cruel Hibernian swines. Eccles: is that you groping behind?

SELLERS: (*Flowerdew voice.*) It'll be a lucky day when I grope your behind, dear.

SECOMBE: Ye-gads! By the light of a flaming cotton bud I beheld an effeminate man with sensible feet and a head to match, carrying a pair of garden shears in a suspicious if fey manner. Out with it, man – what are you doing wielding a gardening tool inside Milligan's noggin?

SELLERS: (*Flowerdew voice.*) I'm his interior barber, dear. I've just been trimming his ear wax. I'm giving his nostril hair a perm at three.

SECOMBE: Now's not the time for hairdressing foibles, man.

SELLERS: (*Flowerdew voice.*) That's a dirty lie. I've never dressed anyone's foibles.

SECOMBE: (*Giggles.*) Needle, nardle, noo! Pull yourself together, sir. I'm journeying to the centre of this brain to discover the source of all Milligan's ills. Which part am I in now?

SELLERS: (*Flowerdew voice.*) You're in moods, dear. If you want to get to the centre you're going to have to nip through depression, turn left at despair, gambol through despondency and take the lift when you get to misery; that'll run you down to desolation – they're a right laugh in desolation – pop past doldrums, dejection, melancholy and gloom; you'll have problems getting through gloom, they're throwing a toga party. Amble past the wreckage of hope, frolic over the bridge of constant sorrow, skip past the ruins of occasional happiness and there you are –

SECOMBE: Where?

SELLERS: (*Flowerdew voice.*) Back where you started. Mush dash. (*Voice fading.*) I'm late for warming up my curling tongs. TTFN.

SECOMBE: Curses! There was only one solution. Desperate times called for desperate means: I was going to have to take a black cab. Aaaaaaaaaaaaaaaaaahhhhhhhhhhhhhhhhhhhhhhhhh!!!!!!!!!

*FX: a taxi pulls up going at a thousand miles an hour. Screeching to a violent halt.*

What kept you? Cabbie: take me to the middle of Milligan's brain.

MILLIGAN: (*Throat voice.*) Sorry mate, don't go south of the ego.

*FX: a taxi pulling away at a thousand miles an hour.*

SECOMBE: Swine!

GREENSLADE: Driven by fear, ambition and an excessive need for lunch our hero Seagoon resorts to the last act of a reckless man: riding the number 14 bus from Lewisham – without a parachute.

*FX: the sound of a Routemaster bus conductor's bell.*

SELLERS: (*Indian conductor's voice.*) Next stop Milligan's brain. Goodness gracious: all change please.

*FX: dramatic 'Quatermass & The Pit' style Sci-Fi music.*

SECOMBE: And so the number 14 bus took me to the epicentre of the tormented mind that churned out Goons scripts for ten and six a go. As I suspected the walls were made of papier-maché, BBC stationary and mush.

MILLIGAN: (*Suppressing a laugh.*) Hello, I'm mush. Has anyone seen my huskies?

SECOMBE: (*Giggles.*) Ying tong iddle I po! At that moment I beheld several be-cloaked Victorian spivs loading Milligan's marbles into a large removal cart. (*Shouts.*) Oi, where you going with those marbles?

SELLERS: (*Grytpype-Thynne voice.*) Greece. Since the English ran off with the last lot they haven't got any of their own.

SECOMBE: Ye-gads! My arch enemy and nemesis!

Hercule Grytpype-Thynne!

SELLERS: (*Grytpype-Thynne voice.*) How dare you call me Hercule Grytpype-Thynne!

SECOMBE: But that's your name.

SELLERS: (*Grytpype-Thynne voice.*) Very well. Under extreme emotional circumstances I'll allow you to use it.

MILLIGAN: (*Moriarty voice.*) All the marbles are on board, your grace.

SECOMBE: Moriarty too! It's wall to wall bounders and cads!

SELLERS: (*Grytpype-Thynne voice.*) Out of my way, Neddie. I like you but I like me more. And there's only one thing I like more than me.

MILLIGAN: (*Moriarty voice.*) Shucks – moi?

SELLERS: (*Grytpype-Thynne voice.*) No – idiot – money and the Greeks will pay a Duke Of Edinburgh's ransom for this lot.

SECOMBE: But if you steal Milligan's marbles he'll be deranged forever. He'll do something unnecessary – like commit suicide or join the Young Conservatives.

SELLERS: (*Grytpype-Thynne voice.*) Don't be a fool! He'd never take the coward's way out and join the Young Conservatives! (*Voice fading.*) Moriarty, beat those oxen and strum that zither! Last one to Athens is a nincompoop!

*FX: galloping oxen's hooves on gravel.*

SECOMBE: (*Shouts.*) Come back! (*Beat.*) They had to be stopped. But how? I tried to think of every effective force at my disposal. And when I ran out of those I thought of the British Army. But where was the nearest unit? But of course! (*Fading.*) Taxi! To the brothels!

GREENSLADE: Thus at Madam Zsa Zsa's Emporium For

Wayward Catholic Girls Neddie found a conveniently galloping Major: scantily clad but raring to go.

SECOMBE: Major Bloodnok!

SELLERS: (*Bloodnok voice.*) It's a lie I tell you! A damn lie! I never touched her! She's my niece! I was teaching her the Heimlich Manoeuvre! I dropped these trousers to help with her circulation! I left that fiver on the dresser to pay for oboe lessons! I demand a court of enquiry!

SECOMBE: That's irrelevant now, Major. Milligan's marbles are heading for the airport in the hands of desperate men. They must be stopped. Now pull up your trousers and behave more like a military man.

SELLERS: (*Bloodnok voice.*) Don't be ridiculous! I was behaving more like a military man with my trousers down.

SECOMBE: Come Major: to Greece! By fastest brewer's dray!

*FX: a long and horrifically sustained donkey fart.*

SELLERS: (*Bloodnok voice.*) That wasn't me I tell you: it was last night's chicken madras!

*FX: The 'Third Man' theme played rabidly.*

GREENSLADE: Thus by paddle steamer and roller-skates Neddie 'Lloyd George Stabbed My Father' Seagoon journeyed to the sun kissed, lotus eating shores of Greece, in search of the Milligan marbles. His only companion? Major Dennis 'It's An Ill Wind' Bloodnok. Whence, on the mean streets of Athens, seeking a cab, they were immediately reminded of home.

*FX: a taxi pulls up at a thousand miles an hour.*

SELLERS: (*Heavy Greek accent.*) Sorry, mate – don't go south of the Acropolis.

*FX: a taxi pulls away a two thousand miles an hour.*

SECOMBE: News from England wasn't good. Milligan without his marbles had turned into a drooling vegetable so moronic he'd applied for the job as quiz show host on *Take Your Pick*. I was running out of time. I needed to restore his mind quickly or face – catastrophe. Imagine my luck when I beheld the wizened forms of Lord and Lady Elgin. The thieving Victorian toe-rags who'd stolen the original marbles from the hallowed halls of mighty Athens and placed them in the lav at the British Museum. Surely they might have some clues. Excuse me gnarled and incontinent gentlefolk –

SELLERS: (*Henry Crun voice.*) Min – Min – he called us gnarled.

MILLIGAN: (*Minnie Bannister voice.*) We're not gnarled you naughty, naughty young man – we're weather-beaten.

SECOMBE: Lady Elgin – you misunderstand –

MILLIGAN: (*Minnie Bannister voice.*) Isn't he portly, Henry? Isn't he a nosher?

SELLERS: (*Henry Crun voice.*) Yes, isn't he rotund, Min?

MILLIGAN: (*Minnie Bannister voice.*) Isn't he corpulent, chubby and fleshy, Henry?

SELLERS: (*Henry Crun voice.*) Isn't he stout, hefty and bloated, Min? Where was he when they introduced rationing?

SECOMBE: In hiding, mate.

SELLERS: (*Henry Crun voice.*) Who ate all the pies? Seagoon ate all the pies. Isn't he obese, Min? Isn't he lard arsed?

MILLIGAN: (*Minnie Bannister voice.*) Yes, Henry, isn't he a fat bastard?

GREENSLADE: Hang about, you can't say that in a Goon

Show, Spike. The BBC will have a fit.

MILLIGAN: Ah, but this isn't a Goon Show. Journey
To The Centre Of Milligan's Brain isn't a genuine,
authentic Goon episode at all. Like a bloody awful soap
opera: this is all just a bad dream.

GREENSLADE: You mean –

MILLIGAN: Yes, it's just a figment of my feverish, crazed
imagination. I'm still in St Luke's, still in bed and still
not allowed sharp implements. This isn't a radio theatre
– (*Points at audience.*) – and that's not a real audience.

SELLERS: (*Bloodnok voice.*) You're telling me.

SECOMBE: I see it now: I've become just a mouth-piece
for the musings of a very sick mind.

MILLIGAN: You were always just a mouth-piece for a
very sick mind.

SECOMBE: But I exist outside of the Goon Show. I must
do otherwise Bernard Delfont wouldn't have booked me
for the Palladium. Twice nightly – matinees Wednesdays
and Saturdays.

SELLERS: (*Bernard Delfont voice.*) The tonsils are fine, boy.
But can you juggle?

MILLIGAN: As the great Secombe you exist outside of my
imagination. (*Laughs darkly.*) But Seagoon is all mine.

SECOMBE: Curses! Trapped I tell you! Trapped inside the
mind of a loony!

MILLIGAN: (*Depressed.*) At least the real Secombe can get
away. I'm trapped in here all the time.

SELLERS: (*Bernard Delfont voice.*) If you can tap-dance
while you're wearing the strait-jacket and throw in some
budgies I can get you a booking for the 12th.

MILLIGAN: You don't get it do you? I've lulled you all

here to kill you. (*Dramatic.*) But first I have to destroy my own marbles.

*FX: the sound of a loud, ticking anarchist's bomb.*

SELLERS: (*Henry Crun voice.*) My God, Min. He's got a bomb!

SECOMBE: You can't destroy your own marbles, man. You'll become an empty zombie.

MILLIGAN: Ah, but empty zombies don't get to write comedy scripts.

SECOMBE: Oh, I don't know, have you met Barry Took? Needle, nardle noo!

MILLIGAN: I say goodbye to you all. Once my marbles have gone none of you will remain: not even me. Hussah for my side!

SELLERS: (*Bloodnok voice.*) Rush him, lads. He has to be stopped.

*FX: a massive explosion of TNT proportions.*

SECOMBE: Too late!

*A huge silence. Then:*

GREENSLADE: Picture it, dear listeners: Milligan's marbles were now but a bloody mush. (*Beat.*) And if I hear another mush joke I'll scream.

MILLIGAN: There. My marbles are no more. Neither are the characters in the – (*Realisation.*) hang on, you're all still here. Greenslade's still announcing. You're all supposed to be gone –

SECOMBE: (*Yells.*) – with the wind!

SELLERS: (*Bloodnok voice.*) It wasn't me I tell you!

SECOMBE: Not that sort of wind: you over-flatulent oaf.

MILLIGAN: You're indestructible. There's only one thing

left to do. I've got to destroy you all with sound effects.

SECOMBE: Not – that. Anything but that!

MILLIGAN: Yes: that. Henry Crun dies in an industrial accident. His genitals crushed by an immense factory mangle.

*FX: the sound of a large factory mangle crushing vulnerable genitalia.*

SELLERS: (*Henry Crun voice.*) My God, Min! He's mangled my gonads –

*FX: the sound of a death rattle.*

SECOMBE: He's killed Henry! The evil, sadistic swine!

MILLIGAN: Minnie Bannister is scalped by Apaches having a bad hair day.

*FX: a blood curdling scream. Followed by a civilised barber's voice: 'And something for the weekend, sir?'*

MILLIGAN: Grytpype-Thynne is raped, pillaged and burnt by gay Vikings.

SELLERS: (*Grytpype-Thynne voice.*) You couldn't just shoot me could you, old chap? Never was keen on gay Vikings. They do rather appalling things with curling tongs you know.

MILLIGAN: (*Firmly.*) By gay Vikings.

*FX: the sound of Vikings singing Norse sea-shanties, quaffing mead, abusing and then burning Grytpype-Thynne to a crisp (merrily).*

SECOMBE: Viking'ed to death. The poor wretch.

MILLIGAN: Little Jim? We drown in a bucket like puppies.

*FX: the sound of a drowning youth gargling the words: 'I've fallen in the water!'.*

MILLIGAN: Eccles? Has a massive heart attack whilst attempting his five times table. It's too much for his under-complicated mind. Bluebottle? Trampled to death by wildebeest in the Transvaal.

SELLERS: (*Bluebottle voice.*) Wildebeest? You dirty rotten –

*FX: the sound of ten thousand wildebeest rushing like the wind across the endless grass of the South African veldt. Managing to trample our favourite boy-scout into small bloody pieces as they do so.*

SECOMBE: Oh, the blood, the pain – he'll never get his pyromaniac badge now.

MILLIGAN: Who's left? Ah, Greenslade.

GREENSLADE: You can't kill me. I've got a contract with the BB –

*FX: a Thompson machine gun fires rapidly. Following by a diving Stuka dropping a bomb on its target, followed by a nuclear explosion a la Hiroshima.*

MILLIGAN: Any questions? Now – Bloodnok.

SELLERS: (*Bloodnok voice.*) I'm not here. Women and Seagoon first. I surrender.

MILLIGAN: Too late. Bloodnok will die by being stung to death by killer bees.

*FX: the sound of bees swarming for the attack.*

Whilst at the same time being sucked to death by rabid aardvarks.

*FX: the sound of mass sucking ant-eaters moving in for the kill.*

SELLERS: (*Bloodnok voice.*) You did say 'sucked' didn't you, old man?

MILLIGAN: On top of which –

(*Bloodnok voice.*) Put me out of my misery, you South London sadist.

MILLIGAN: Unleash the hounds of hell!

*FX: the sound of bees swarming, ant eaters sucking and the hounds of hell ripping Bloodnok limb from limb. Followed by a loud and satisfied – belch.*

SECOMBE: Bloodnok, alas, poor Bloodnok. Save for having the digestive system of a wart hog he wasn't all bad.

MILLIGAN: For the minor characters in the Goon Show cannon? I wish them mass pestilence, the plague and the Black Death – all rolled into one.

*FX: mass weeping, gnashing of teeth, boils bursting and bodies hitting mud.*

*Music: a quick burst of 'The Funeral March'.*

Which leaves only: Seagoon.

SECOMBE: You can't kill Seagoon. He's the only character I play. It's alright for Sellers bounding manfully through the valley of the accents –

MILLIGAN: He has to die. You've needled your last noo.

SECOMBE: At the risk of repeating myself ad infinitum: curses!

MILLIGAN: His end? Zulus.

SECOMBE: What, what, what? You can't mean –

MILLIGAN: Yes. They're itching to get at you. After the Welsh cruelly slaughtered them at Rourke's Drift. Any last requests?

SECOMBE: A ten yard start?

MILLIGAN: Too late.

*FX: the sound of the massed ranks of the Zulu hordes*

*swarming towards Secombe.*

SECOMBE: (*Sings.*) Men of Harlech –
Aaaaaaaaaaaaahhhhhhhhhhhhhhhh!!!!

*FX: the sound of a Zulu warrior victory dance. Dancing on the spear-strewn corpse of Seagoon.*

*The sound fades to silence.*

MILLIGAN: All dead. All of them. No marbles, no Goon characters, I'm free, free at bloody last. It's the Lewisham Labour Exchange for me.

*A long silence. SECOMBE coughs.*

SECOMBE: We hate to spoil your solitude.

SELLERS: But rumours of our death have been greatly exaggerated.

GREENSLADE: Like General MacArthur and the average bounced cheque: we have returned.

MILLIGAN: (*Desperate.*) What do I have to bloody do to lose you stinking bastards?

SECOMBE: You can't stop your brain thinking, Spike. Or being funny. It was why you were born.

MILLIGAN: I don't want to be funny. I've been funny too long. I just want to live.

GREENSLADE: But that's why we've come back. Killing us would kill you too.

MILLIGAN: Look: sod this metaphysical mumbo jumbo. Just get out of my bloody –

*FX: the sounds of a distant battle.*

What's that?

SECOMBE: What's what?

MILLIGAN: There's shelling.

SELLERS: Of course there is.

MILLIGAN: I didn't order that special effect.

SELLERS: No, it ordered you. You're not in charge of this dream any more, Milligan.

MILLIGAN: (*Worried.*) I'm not?

SECOMBE: No. It's time to go back, Spike.

MILLIGAN: Back where?

SECOMBE: You know where.

GREENSLADE: It's for the best, old son.

SELLERS: (*Pearly Gates voice.*) Physician heal thyself and all caper:

MILLIGAN: You can't re-write my dream. It's not allowed.

SECOMBE: It is now.

GREENSLADE: Check your contract:

SELLERS: (*Groucho Marx voice.*) Particularly the sanity clause.

*FX: the noises of battle get louder.*

MILLIGAN: I don't want to do this.

SECOMBE: No choice, boy. The creatures in your head have taken over.

SELLERS: (*Italian voice.*) Time to return to Old Italy.

SECOMBE: One last time.

MILLIGAN: I can't –

*MILLIGAN climbs back into bed afraid.*

GREENSLADE: (*NCO voice.*) There's no such thing as can't in the British Army, Gunner Milligan.

MILLIGAN: You can't talk to me like that. I'm not in the –

GREENSLADE: (*NCO voice.*) Explain why you're not in uniform, soldier. And explain it fast. Jim-jams? I'll give you bleedin' jim-jams!

MILLIGAN: (*Faraway.*) I'd been on duty seventy hours when I volunteered. To take ammunition up Mount Dimiano.

GREENSLADE: (*NCO voice.*) Fighting a war isn't a nine 'til five job, soldier. You can't run home to mummy.

MILLIGAN: I was hit by a mortar, wounded in the leg.

GREENSLADE: (*NCO voice.*) Merely a flesh wound, soldier. Gangrene is a cheap excuse for shirkers.

MILLIGAN: Carried to a medical station, bandaged up, given a couple of pills and sent on my way: despite the shell shock.

GREENSLADE: (*NCO voice.*) Shell shock? Poppycock. If everyone was shocked by shells we'd never have a decent war.

MILLIGAN: There's no such thing as a 'decent' fucking war.

SECOMBE: (*Softly.*) Who ever said there was, boy?

MILLIGAN: I was never the same person after: sobbing, stammering, jumping every time a gun was fired –

GREENSLADE: (*NCO voice.*) What's this, soldier? Whining for England again?

MILLIGAN: So with all the compassion they could muster they court-martialled me.

GREENSLADE: (*NCO voice.*) For unreasonable behaviour, soldier. You're British. You can't show emotion. You should be like Jack Hawkins in *The Cruel Sea*: all duffle-coat, cocoa and firmly clenched buttocks:

MILLIGAN: (*Yells.*) Fuck firmly clenched buttocks.

SELLERS: (*Worried.*) Do we have to?

MILLIGAN: If it'd been World War One they would have shot me.

GREENSLADE: (*NCO voice.*) We might bleedin' yet, soldier. We might just bleedin' yet. Exits left with vein on neck throbbing, parade ground butch and twice as perky.

*FX: the noise of war and battle fades.*

SECOMBE: You can't destroy yourself thinking about it, Milligan.

SELLERS: You did better than most: mentioned in dispatches in North Africa.

SECOMBE: A brave man.

MILLIGAN: Brave? I fell apart at the seams. I've never been together since. All the king's horses and all the king's men couldn't put Milligan together again.

GREENSLADE: You don't have to be together.

SELLERS: You don't even have to be strong.

SECOMBE: Life isn't a John Wayne movie: all blood, guts and machismo.

MILLIGAN: It's not?

SECOMBE: You're too hard on yourself. You always were.

GREENSLADE: You tried your best. What more can a man do?

MILLIGAN: (*Surprised.*) Nothing:

SECOMBE: Precisely.

*A silence. MILLIGAN blinks around him. Unfocused, confused.*

MILLIGAN: Is this dream over?

SECOMBE: Just about. But you've a song to sing.

MILLIGAN: Song? Which song?

GREENSLADE: You know which song, Spike.

MILLIGAN: (*Quietly.*) Oh, that one.

SELLERS: Yes.

MILLIGAN: 'The soft underbelly of Europe'. That's what Churchill called Italy. They died in their thousands to prove him wrong. And so we sang the song. We sang it beside the graves of the dead at Monte Cassino. We sang it on the troop ships taking the body bags home. We sang it at night scared in trenches, in bars and brothels, drunk or maudlin or both. We sang it in the field hospitals and the dressing stations amongst the wounded and the dying and the maimed. The men who survived Italy will sing it to their dying day.

*MILLIGAN sings softly to the tune of 'Lily Marlene':*

MILLIGAN: (*Sings.*) Look across the mountains
In the wind and rain,
See the wooden crosses,
Some that bear no name.
Heart-break and toil
And suffering gone,
The lads beneath them
Slumber on
The lucky D-Day dodgers
Who'll stay in Italy.

*As he sings he lies back in bed. The lights slowly fade to black as he sings. When they rise again only SECOMBE remains. Standing over the bed.*

SECOMBE: Spike? Are you awake?

MILLIGAN: (*Sitting up.*) Oh. Hello.

SECOMBE: You were singing *D-Day Dodgers.*

MILLIGAN: I was?

SECOMBE: In your sleep. I haven't heard that song in fifteen years.

MILLIGAN: I had a dream.

SECOMBE: A bad one?

MILLIGAN: Not altogether. Where's Doctor Hampton?

SECOMBE: (*Grins.*) As in Huge-Hampton?

MILLIGAN: No, Harry, my psychiatrist. The one who looks like Greenslade.

SECOMBE: Your psychiatrist is Doctor Farber, Spike. Unless Greenslade is a fifty year old Israeli woman with child bearing hips and an arse the size of China you're imagining things again.

MILLIGAN: Shame. He was the only mirage I ever liked.

*A silence.*

SECOMBE: The BBC called. About the show's demise.

MILLIGAN: They took it badly. When I told them. I knew they would.

SECOMBE: Screw 'em. We had a good run: nine years. Time to move on.

MILLIGAN: Yes. (*Beat.*) Sorry.

SECOMBE: What's there to be sorry about? Radio's had its day. It's all aboard the goggle-box these days. I'll miss Goon Sundays though.

MILLIGAN: Yes. (*Beat.*) How's work?

SECOMBE: Got my nose to the grindstone, boy. There's always need for a tenor. (*Beat.*) What'll you get up too?

MILLIGAN: I thought I might try television.

SECOMBE: You told me once you couldn't do television.

'Cause you can't paint surreal pictures like radio.

MILLIGAN: Maybe it's time someone tried.

SECOMBE: If it has an audience of one: I'll be the one.

MILLIGAN: Why are you so good to me?

SECOMBE: (*Grins.*) 'Cause deep down? You're a Welshman, boy.

MILLIGAN: Another race? That's all I need.

SECOMBE: You are okay aren't you, Spike? Better, you know –

MILLIGAN: So they tell me. A bit scared. I walk Goonless now.

SECOMBE: You may think you walk alone, boy. But you don't, you know. I'll always be there. So will Sellers in his own way. One for all and all for one; Goons forever and all that.

MILLIGAN: Do you think?

SECOMBE: I know it.

MILLIGAN: I'll have to start again from scratch. I've been thinking of starting a book. But I can't think what to write.

SECOMBE: What was the biggest thing that ever happened to you, Spike?

MILLIGAN: The war I suppose.

SECOMBE: No suppose about it.

MILLIGAN: What about it?

SECOMBE: You ever read any war books, Spike?

MILLIGAN: Not many. I was trying to forget.

SECOMBE: All the books I read were written by generals. The blokes who pushed dots around a map, miles behind the front. Wouldn't it be nice to read something by one of the dots?

MILLIGAN: Dots?

*SECOMBE stands to attention.*

SECOMBE: What was your name before the war, Gunner Milligan?

MILLIGAN: Terry.

SECOMBE: And after it?

MILLIGAN: Spike.

SECOMBE: Anybody call you Terry now?

MILLIGAN: No.

SECOMBE: Precisely. The war made people like us, boy. What was the Goons if it wasn't an attack on every pompous twit officer we ever met? Write about what made you, boy. For dots like me, for dots like you, for all the dots who never came home.

*A silence. Then SECOMBE snaps to attention and gives MILLIGAN a smart military salute.*

Permission to tell you I love you, Gunner Milligan?

MILLIGAN: (*Saluting him back.*) Go forth and multiply, Gunner Secombe.

*SECOMBE laughs, blows a huge raspberry and exits. A pause. MILLIGAN mutters in thought:*

Dots...

*Suddenly a blinding, heavenly light hits the typewriter on the nurse's desk. A celestial choir begins to sing: 'I was glad, glad when the Lord said to me...' MILLIGAN gets up and staggers towards the light as if he's a cripple who's just been cured by Jesus. He sits at the desk. The light from heaven shines like a beacon as MILLIGAN begins to slowly type:*

Adolf...Hitler...my...part...in...his...downfall...

*A beat. MILLIGAN stares at the page before him then looks up and cries:*

Eureka!

*The lights change.*

*Music: the 'Q' series theme.*

*The lights rise on a Goon Show (we presume). MILLIGAN, SECOMBE, SELLERS and GREENSLADE stand before their respective microphones:*

GREENSLADE: Back from the depths of Valhalla, enter Peter Sellers; riding a troll, the hard way.

SELLERS: (*Bluebottle voice.*) So tell me, Eccles, whatever became of our brave band of broadcasting brothers?

MILLIGAN: (*Eccles voice.*) You made the best anti-war film of all time: *Doctor Strangelove.* Became an international film star. Then had a massive heart attack whilst making love to your gorgeous, scantily clad Swedish wife. Corrrrr.

SELLERS: (*Bluebottle voice.*) Did I become deaded?

MILLIGAN: (*Eccles voice.*) No, you survived to make a come-back as Inspector Clouseau. Becoming a box-office sensation.

SELLERS: (*Inspector Clouseau voice.*) Does your dog bite?

MILLIGAN: (*Eccles voice.*) You died aged fifty five after making *Being There.* The film you believed to be your masterpiece.

SELLERS: (*Bluebottle voice.*) But was Bluebottle happy?

MILLIGAN: (*Eccles voice.*) Not particularly.

SELLERS: (*Bluebottle voice.*) Gosh darn it. Foiled by the fates once again.

GREENSLADE: On a lighter note they played your

request at your funeral.

*Music: a burst of 'In The Mood'.*

SECOMBE: But what of me? Secombe the sturdy? What became of Seagoon?

MILLIGAN: You lived to a ripe old age. Happily married to the same woman for fifty three years.

SELLERS: (*Secombe voice.*) Friend to monarchs and morons alike. Loved by all save for critics of the God slot.

SECOMBE: Three cheers for Wales!

GREENSLADE: You also had two top ten hits: *If I Ruled The World* and *This Is My Song*. And were rather touching as Mr Bumble in the musical film of *Oliver*.

SELLERS: (*Grytpype-Thynne voice.*) You became a veritable pillar of the community. A stalwart of society. (*Churchill voice.*) While Secombe stands – so stands the Bank of England. When Secombe falls –

SECOMBE: They have a minor earthquake in Swansea. (*Giggles.*) Needle nardle noo!

GREENSLADE: And Greenslade? The ever patient, dignified announcer?

MILLIGAN: Died in a toilet in 1961. Heart attack.

GREENSLADE: Charming.

MILLIGAN: It was alright. It was a pub toilet. You died as you wanted to go; with a drink in your hand.

GREENSLADE: Well, that's alright then. He said ironically.

SECOMBE: But wait – what of Gunner Milligan? The hero of this far fetched, far flung tale?

SELLERS: (*Grytpype-Thynne voice.*) Took to television. Wrote the 'Q' series. Changed comedy as we know it. Influenced a generation. Blah-blah, drone-drone, yawn, stream of z's. (*Feigns sleep.*) Zzzzzzzzzzzzz....

*Music: a burst of Monty Python Theme/The Liberty Bell.*

(*Grytpype-Thynne voice.*) And called the heir to the throne a grovelling little bastard.

GREENSLADE: Was he beheaded?

MILLIGAN: Worse, they knighted me – the sadists.

SECOMBE: You got custody of your children and brought them up to believe in fairies in the garden, love for the world and humanity for all mankind. Marrying three times to beautiful women.

SELLERS: (*Willium voice.*) In spite of looking like a scarecrow with the mange.

GREENSLADE: And of what, we ask indifferently, was Milligan most proud?

MILLIGAN: I never joined an establishment I despised. I never accepted my place in a country that demands you have one. I never let the bastards grind me down.

SECOMBE: And were the Goons re-united in show business heaven?

SELLERS: (*Willium voice.*) Save it for the God slot, mush.

MILLIGAN: Well, were we?

GREENSLADE: Answers on a postcard to: British Broadcasting House, Lower Penge, Botswana, Norway. But now a party political broadcast on behalf of the Milligan Party.

MILLIGAN: Bring back National Service! And if in doubt – shoot it!

SELLERS: (*Bloodnok voice.*) By God he's solved inflation!

SECOMBE: (*Yells.*) What about the workers!

GREENSLADE: And so folks, we say goodnight from happydom. Good luck, God bless and last but certainly least –

ALL: (*Shout together.*) Ying Tong!

*Music begins: SELLERS, SECOMBE, MILLIGAN and GREENSLADE sing: 'The Ying Tong Song'. The song ends. A blackout. The lights rise. The cast march on, salute rather than bow and exit as the lights fade once more to black.*